EASY TO EMBROIDER

EASY TO EMBROIDER

Anna Griffiths

Series consultant: Eve Harlow

ANAYA PUBLISHERS LTD LONDON

First published in Great Britain in 1991
by Anaya Publishers Ltd, Strode House, Osnaburgh Street,
London NW1 3ND

Editor Eve Harlow
Designer Mike Leaman
Photographer Di Lewis
Illustrator Kate Simunek
Artwork Julie Ward

British Library Cataloguing in Publication Data

Griffiths, Anna
Easy to embroider.—(Easy to make)
1. Embroidery.   Embroidery
I. Title   II. Series
746.443
ISBN 1 85470-038-3

Typeset by Tradespools Limited, Frome, Somerset, UK

Colour Reproduction by Columbia Offset, Singapore

Printed and bound in Great Britain by Clays Ltd, Bungay, Suffolk, UK

CONTENTS

Introduction

The gentle art of embroidery has survived for centuries in almost every part of the world. This ageless craft, springing from a desire to decorate clothing and furnishings with colour and patterns, still uses stitches that were popular 2000 years ago.

Embroidery is a most soothing and relaxing occupation and one which can be learned and enjoyed at any age. Very little equipment is needed to practise the craft – just some threads, a needle and some fabric. You can add other pieces of equipment – such as an embroidery hoop – later.

Although there are hundreds of embroidery stitches, you need to know only a few to use this book. I have intentionally kept the number of different stitches used to the minimum. You'll find them simple to work as most of them are based on straight stitches – running stitch, backstitch, and cross stitch for example. These three stitches are used in the chapter 'Going Straight'.

In 'Kid's stuff', the designs are simple and appealing for childrens' clothing and pictures. In 'Little Gifts' there are items for bazaars which can be made quickly and inexpensively, including simple cards, pot-pourri bags and other pretty things that will help to boost funds.

'Home makers' has many lovely things to make – bright place mats and napkins and stylish towels to brighten dull mornings.

In 'Fashion extras' motifs have been used on some unusual things – a prayer book cover and a shawl for instance.

Standard, easily obtained fabrics have been chosen for the projects – gingham, felt, cotton and linen. Always wash fabrics before you use them to remove any dressing or stiffening. Felt should be damp-pressed to settle the fibres and encourage any shrinkage that might occur.

The embroidery threads most used – stranded cottons and wools – are well-known brands with a wide distribution.

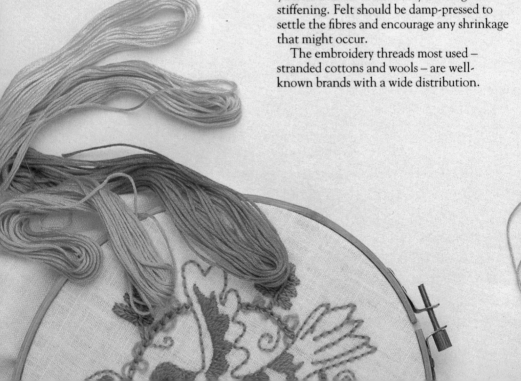

Should you have any difficulty obtaining either fabrics or threads some mail order addresses are given on page 96.

Needles are important pieces of equipment and you will need a selection of types and sizes.

Crewel needles: These have long eyes to take one or more threads and come in sizes 1–10.

Tapestry needles: These are blunt-ended with large eyes to slip between canvas and evenweave fabric threads without splitting them. They come in sizes 18–24.

Chenille needles: These are short with large eyes and a sharp point and are used for embroidery with thick yarns. They come in sizes 18–24.

Embroidery hoops and frames are essential for some projects in this book, and once you become used to working with them your stitches will be far more even. Choose a round hoop for small projects in surface embroidery and a frame for canvas or large embroideries.

Most people regard a personal, hand-made gift as very special, for it is a generous act of giving, both of time and creativity. If you feel apprehensive about working a large, complex piece, but still want to make something with embroidery, then this book is for you. You will find that there are lots of easy things to make and others that take a little more time and care.

Some of the designs were worked for me by friends who are not professional embroiderers, so it was the ideal gauge for me to see if beginners could do them fairly easily. And, who knows, perhaps working something from this book will inspire you to go on to bigger, more ambitious designs. If this happens, I shall have succeeded in all I set out to do.

Transferring designs
Two methods of transferring designs to fabric are used mainly in this book. The first involves dressmakers' carbon paper. This is placed between the pattern and fabric, then the lines are traced over. The second method uses an embroidery transfer pencil. The traced pattern is drawn over on the wrong side of the paper. Then the pattern is ironed onto the fabric. The direct tracing method is also described (see page 42) and so is the basting thread technique (page 26). For most fabrics, you will find the dressmakers' carbon paper or the embroidery transfer pencil methods the easiest.

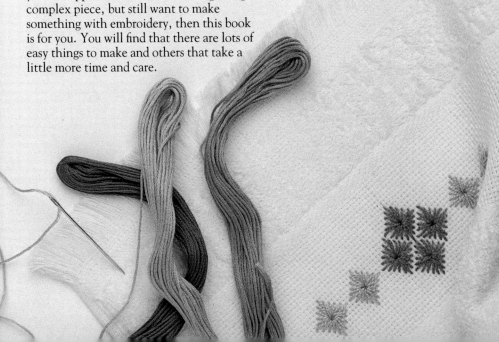

1: GOING STRAIGHT

Making Waves

One of the easiest ways of working embroidery is on fabrics which already have a pattern, like these spotted curtains. They have been pattern-darned with thick red thread. The idea could be used in other ways, white on white for instance, or in pastel shades.

Materials

Spotted voile net curtain fabric (calculate the amount as twice the width of the window, with the depth adjusted to suit your window, plus turnings)

DMC Coton Perle no 5 (colour of choice)

A sharp crewel needle (with a big eye to take the thread easily).

Preparation

1 Stitch the sides of the curtain. Leave the top and bottom edges.

Working the embroidery

2 Start the first line of embroidery at least 6in (15cm) from the bottom. Make a small knot at one end of the thread and push the knot inside the sewn side seam to 'lose' it.

3 With running stitches, darn from the edge of one spot to the near edge of the next one, take the needle down, come up the other side of the spot and continue to work the pattern. On the back you should only see stitches the width of the spot.

Work the wave design about 6in (15cm) from the curtain's bottom edge.

Finishing

4 Turn up the hem and hand sew with small stitches. Finish the top edge for whatever hanging system you are using.

There are lots of possibilities with this simple technique; more than one colour could be used, or random-dyed threads could look effective. Ideally the thread and the fabric should be compatible, especially for items that have to be continually laundered. Avoid small areas of embroidery where you have to repeatedly join and finish the thread off. It can look messy on a sheer fabric.

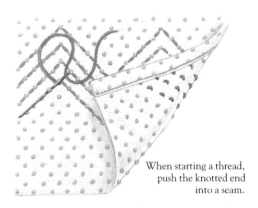

When starting a thread, push the knotted end into a seam.

Pretty in gingham

This clever, but simple, technique – called Swiss embroidery – is both pretty and practical. Here it is used for a table mat, but it can be used to decorate all kinds of household articles made of gingham.

Materials

Evenly-checked gingham, 10in (25cm) square
White cotton fabric the same size
Coloured basting thread
Crochet cotton no 5 or no 8
Sharp crewel needle.

Preparation

1 Using soft cotton, baste the outer area of the finished mat. Work along the outside edges of dark and half-toned squares so that you have a working area of $9^{1}/_{2}$in (24cm) square – (39 × 39 dark and half-toned squares).

Working the embroidery

2 Work the foundation threads two squares in from the marked edges.

3 Lay the vertical foundation threads by taking the needle under the white squares and over the half-toned squares, making the stitches absolutely central on the squares. Repeat this horizontally.

4 Bring the needle and thread out at the top edge of the top right dark square and work two fly stitches in it, one on top of the other (see diagrams a, b, c, d).

5 Bring the needle through again (see d) and, without putting the needle into the fabric again, pass the needle under the foundation threads twice, so that you outline the white square with threads (see diagrams e–f). Take the needle down into the fabric and bring it up at the corner of the next dark square to the left ready to make the next two fly stitches. Continue in this way, until the grid is covered with embroidery (see picture).

Finishing

6 Place the white backing fabric to the embroidery, right sides facing. Machine-stitch from the middle of one side, round three sides and part of the fourth. Turn right side out, press. Close the open seam with slip stitches. Edge with bought lace.

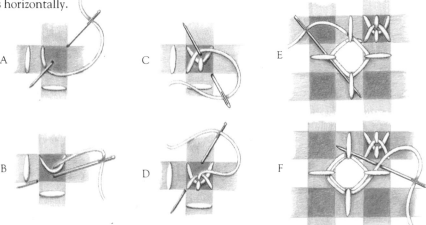

Fly stitch
Work two fly stitches, one on top of the other (a–d).

Outline the white squares with threads passed under the foundation threads (e–f).

Smart cooks

A smart crisp apron like this will make you feel very professional in the kitchen. The apron top and the pocket are decorated with Swiss embroidery in crochet cotton, a technique that can be used effectively on many other articles.

Materials
(Finished size 33 × 25in (82.5 × 62.5cm)
Adjust fabric quantity if a different size is
  required.)
Gingham with an even check, 1¼ yd
  (1.7m) × 36in (90cm)
3⅜ yd (3m) red bias binding
White crochet cotton no 5.

Preparation
1 Cut a strip 4½ × 20in (11 × 51cm) for the neckband and two strips 2½ × 23in (6 × 57.5cm) for the ties. Fold each strip lengthways, wrong sides facing, and stitch ¼in (6mm) in from the edge along the length. Turn to the right side and press so that the seam is centred on the neckband and ties.

2 Fold the remaining fabric in half. Using chalk pencil and a ruler mark out the half apron shape, following the diagram. Cut out. From the cut-away, cut the pocket 8 × 5in (20 × 13cm). Curve the bottom corners as shown in the diagram.

Working the embroidery
3 Referring to the technique on page 12, and working from the charts given here, lay the foundation threads for the embroidery on the pocket piece and on the apron bib.

4 Complete the embroidery as described on page 12, working fly stitches as indicated on the diagrams given here.

Making up the apron
5 Fold over 5in (12.5cm) allowance at the top of the apron to the wrong side. Turn a narrow hem, press and slip stitch neatly.

6 Turn the allowance on the top edge of the pocket and finish in the same way. Neaten the pocket edges with bias binding.

7 Finish the edges of the apron with bias binding then pin, baste and machine-stitch the pocket in position. Fold the ends of the necktie and stitch to the apron top. Stitch the side ties in place, turn in the ends of the ties and stitch.

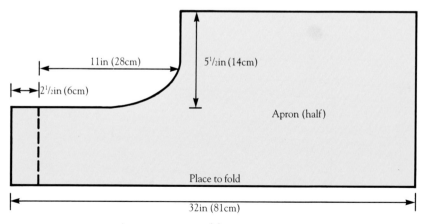

11in (28cm)　　5½in (14cm)

2½in (6cm)

Apron (half)

Place to fold

32in (81cm)

Pocket chart

Stitch ties, right sides facing, then press with seam centred.

Bib chart

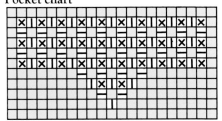

KEY

⊠ Foundation threads

⊟ Double fly stitches

Traditional Japanese

Sashiko embroidery, where formal patterns are worked in simple, regular, running stitches, was originally used to hold layers of fabric together for extra warmth. Here it is used decoratively.

Working the embroidery

1 Trace the desired pattern directly onto the fabric, using an embroidery pencil. If preferred, use dressmakers' carbon paper.

2 Work with a 20in (50cm)-length of embroidery thread and make a knot at the end. If you are using more than one thickness of fabric, slide the knot between the layers so that it cannot be seen.

3 Work small, even, running stitches along the design lines. With a little practice you will be able to pick up several stitches on the needle, equally spaced, before pulling it through. This makes the work a lot quicker to do. You should do this only on straight lines. On curves, work individual stitches.

Running stitch worked along straight lines.

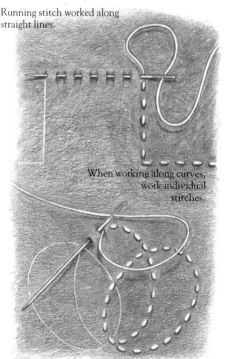

When working along curves, work individual stitches.

The Sashiko technique is ideal for decorating – and quilting – fabrics for clothes and accessories.

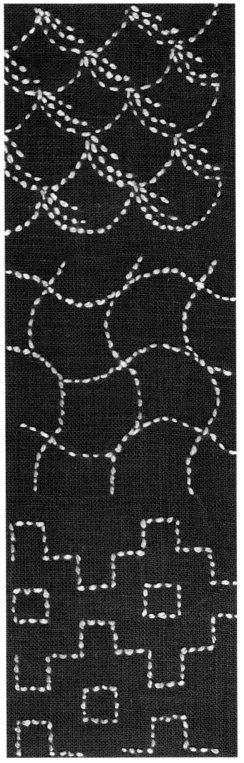

Sashiko can be worked inside shapes or freely worked as decoration on yokes, pockets etc. Work embroidery before making up the garment.

City landscape

Only three stitches have been used for this picture, but the variety of threads in a limited colour range, plus the use of ribbons and beads, makes this an exciting project even for beginners. The canvas is allowed to show in some areas, adding texture to the design.

Materials

Finished size 7 × 6in (18 × 15cm)
White single thread canvas 14 holes to 1in (2.5cm), 9 × 8in (23 × 20cm)
DMC Coton perle no 3 in the following colours: lilac 208, white, grey 318, green 503, almond green 504, lemon 3078, dark green 501
DMC stranded cotton, 1 skein of each of apricot 353 and orange 977
A few glass beads, pearl and pale green, 2mm in diameter
White net 1¼ × 9in (3 × 23cm)
White rayon thread
White, double-faced satin ribbon ⅛th (3mm) wide, 18in (45cm)
Tapestry needle
Small embroidery frame (optional).

Preparation

1 Put the canvas in the frame, or cover the edges with masking tape to prevent fraying.

Working the embroidery

2 The key alongside the picture indicates the colours and stitches and you should work each section completely before moving on to the next one.

3 On the central beaded area, the white net is basted across the width before the stitches are worked. Remove these at the end. Thread the beads onto the needle at the beginning of each downward stitch. The number you put on and the thread colour order can be re-arranged to fill the space as you wish.

4 Quite a lot of the stitches used allow the canvas to show through and this adds to the texture. Do not be tempted to fill in more solidly or it will look heavy and overworked.

5 Two lines have white ribbon underneath them. Lay the ribbon across the canvas in a straight line and take the ends through to the back. Stitch the ends behind. Work cross stitches over the ribbon.

KEY

A – lilac 208 – straight stitches over 1 thread ———

B – grey 318 – cross stitch over 5 threads both ways with ——— small centre cross over 1 thread

C – white – French knots with extended tails ———

D – grey 318 – straight stitch ———

E – lilac 208 – cross stitch worked over ribbon ———

F – white – herringbone over 8 threads, with 1 row grey ——— 318 cross stitch underneath over 3 threads.

G – grey 318 – cross stitch over 3 threads ———
A – lilac 208 – straight stitches over 1 thread ———

H – net over 18 threads plus random lines ——— of beads and threads

A – orange 977 – straight stitches over 1 thread ———

B – almond 504 – cross stitch over 5 threads both ways with small centre cross over 1 thread ———

C – apricot 352 French knots with extended tails ———

D – almond 504 straight stitch ———
E – orange 977 – cross stitch worked over ribbon ———

F – dark green 501 herringbone over 8 threads with 1 row lemon 3078 underneath

G – lemon 3078 cross stitch over 3 threads ———
A – orange 977 – straight stitches over 1 thread ———

6 When the embroidery is complete you may need to pull it into shape slightly before it is mounted and framed. Pin it to an ironing board in as perfect a rectangle as possible, then hold a steam iron just above it for a few seconds. Leave the work until really dry before removing.

For this type of embroidery, all kinds of yarns and threads can be mixed together to good effect. You might try novelty knitting yarns, crochet cottons or even metallic threads. Some of these are multi-coloured and, with beads, will produce glittering effects. Parcel string, frayed-out rope and non-woven gift ribbons of different types could make interesting textural contrast, especially when used with narrow satin ribbons.

Quilted fan

This elegant fabric brooch is worked with only two embroidery stitches, French knots and backstitch, but the clever use of beads and gold thread makes it look very sophisticated.

Materials

Black silk-type fabric, $13^1/_2 \times 8$in
  (34×20cm)
Polyester wadding $^3/_8$in (9mm) thick, 2
  pieces 8in (20cm) square
Medium-weight black cotton fabric, 8in
  (20cm) square
Anchor Pearl cotton no 5, 1 skein Black 0403
Anchor Stranded cotton, 1 skein Black 0403
Mez Effektgarn metallic thread, 1 spool
  Gold 300
43 grey beads 2mm wide
Stiff card 4in (10cm) square
A small safety pin
Crewel needles nos 5 and 7.

Preparation

1 Cut a piece of the silky black fabric 8in (20cm) square.

2 Trace the fan design on thin paper and transfer to the centre of the right side of the fabric.

3 Place the two layers of wadding together with the silky fabric on top and the cotton fabric underneath. Baste through all the layers using long stitches in lines 2in (5cm) apart.

Working the embroidery

4 Using the size no 7 needle and the gold thread, work backstitches along the fan pattern lines. Work the stitches through all layers taking the needle vertically down into the fabric for every stitch.

5 Work French knots with one thickness of black pearl cotton.

6 Sew beads between the French knots with one strand of black stranded cotton.

Making up the brooch

7 Remove the basting stitches. Trim the fabric back to within $^3/_4$in (2cm) of the finished size of the brooch.

8 Cut card to the fan shape. Use the pattern to cut another fan shape from the remaining silk fabric with $^1/_2$in (12mm) all round for seam allowance.

9 Place the card on the wrong side of the padded embroidery, then put the backing on the card. Turn in the seam allowances and hem neatly all round.

Finishing

10 Cut 20 lengths of stranded cotton 6in (15cm) long, fold in half and tie through the middle. Bind round just below this with cotton to form the tassel. Stitch to the bottom point of the brooch and trim back to $2^1/_2$in (6cm) length. Sew a safety pin to the brooch back.

KEY
1 – Backstitch in gold
2 – Bead
3 – French Knot

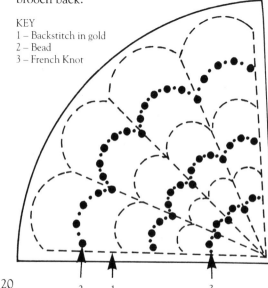

Quilting the fabric:
Take needle vertically
down through all layers

Bring needle up vertically
through fabric to
complete the back stitch

Fold the bunch of threads in half, then tie in middle,
then below the 'head' to form a tassel.

2: KID'S STUFF

Buttoned-up

Work a little embroidery around a novelty button and you have a garment with an immediate talking point! A round button can be made into a flower, little boats can be put on the high seas and trains steam along puffing smoke.

Materials
A ready-made garment
Novelty buttons
Small amounts of stranded cotton in various
  colours.

Preparation
1 Remove the existing buttons. Lay the novelty button in place over the buttonhole and, with a sharply pointed pencil, lightly mark the desired design on the fabric. The trace-off patterns given here are for you to use with buttons similar to those pictured. If you are using the patterns, trace them and transfer onto the garment, using dressmakers' carbon paper. Repeat the chosen design on all the buttonholes.

Working the embroidery

LITTLE BOATS
2 Using two strands of embroidery thread, work the waves in blue stem stitch, the sun's rays with yellow straight stitches and the centre in satin stitch. The two birds in the sky are white, straight stitches.

3 When the embroidery is completed, sew on the buttons.

PUFFING TRAINS
4 Using two strands of embroidery cotton work the puffs of smoke in white satin stitch, the tender truck in yellow satin stitch with blue back stitches along the top edge. The wheels are worked with grey stem stitches.

> **Button ideas**
> **Windmills** Work small clouds and lines for water.
> **Dog** Work a lead from the dog's head.
> **Cat** Perhaps a ball of wool or a mouse.
> **Aeroplane** Three or four clouds.
> **Icecream cone** Lazy-daisy flowers all round.
> **Little cars** Clouds of dust behind the car.
> **Ladybird** Work a big flower shape all round.
> **Butterfly** Work a sun and clouds.
> **Pencils** Embroider crossed lines in different colours.
> **Ruler** Embroider numbers all round.

Trace these patterns and transfer to the fabric around the buttonholes

Happy feet

Cotton espadrilles, or canvas slippers, are favourite summer footwear for young and old alike. With painted decorations and a little embroidery you can make them extra special.

Materials
Fabric shoes
Fabric paint pens
Cotton perle or soft cotton embroidery
  threads
Short needle with a large eye.

Preparation
1 Copy the design from the picture on to the shoe upper, using soft, light-coloured pencil. Paint the designs and leave to dry.

2 Put your hand inside the slippers to see how far you can comfortably work, taking a needle in and out of the fabric. You may decide to keep the area of embroidery close to the edges.

Working the embroidery
3 Chain stitch and straight stitch have been used on the shoes pictured. Embellish the painted areas in the same way, or use stitches and thread colours of your choice.

Motifs from children's stencil kits can be used to decorate shoes. Dab the colour on, holding the stencil firmly in place. Embroider along outlines or add details. Beads can also be sewn on.
  To put a name on the shoes, draw the letters on paper first then baste over the outlines with thread. Tear off the paper gently leaving the threads on the fabric as your embroidery guide.

Stitch library

Cross stitch

The stitches shown here are ideal for working on canvas and other fabrics

Herringbone stitch

Blanket stitch

Couching

Detached chain stitch

26

Rocking horse

This delightful, three-dimensional rocking horse is used on a pinafore dress and a matching drawstring bag, but it would also look good on the front of a sweater or on a school rucksack. Wherever it is used it will be well-loved by the wearer.

Materials

Ready-made pinafore (or dress)
Piece of yellow, lightweight, cotton fabric 19½in (50cm) square
Blue, lightweight, cotton fabric 4½in (12cm) square
23½in (60cm) of white, double face satin ribbon ¼in (6mm) wide
47in (120cm) piping cord
9½ × 4½in (24 × 12cm) Bondaweb
Anchor stranded cotton 1 skein each of delphinium 0120, hyacinth 0940, maize 0943
Anchor Tapisserie wool, 1 skein of snuff brown 3064
Crewel needle.

Preparation

1 Trace the outline of the horse and transfer to 4½in (12cm) square of the yellow fabric. Iron a piece of Bondaweb to the wrong side of the fabric.

2 Cut away the excess fabric round the horse and between the stirrup and rocker.

Peel the paper backing from the Bondaweb and iron the shape to the front of the pinafore.

Working the embroidery

3 Follow the key for colours and stitches. Three strands of embroidery cotton are used throughout. Begin with the satin stitch areas. Work stem stitches over the outlines so that the stitches cover the edges of the fabric.

4 To make the mane and tail, cut the skein of wool through the loops at each end. Put half on one side for the bag. Cut 2 pieces of ribbon 6in (15cm) long. Tie one piece in a bow round on one end of the remaining half-skein, about ¾in (18mm) from the end. Divide the wool strands in 3 and plait. Tie a second ribbon bow ¾in (18mm) from the end.

5 Sew on the mane and tail along the horse's forehead, neck and back, using small stitches, and matching thread to fabric.

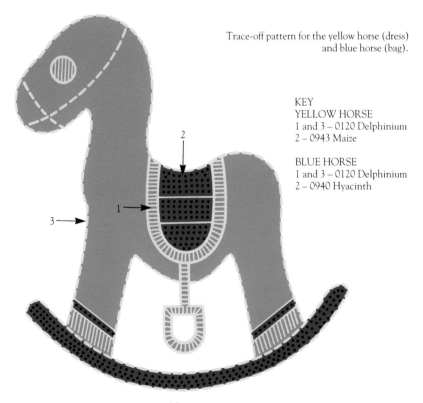

Trace-off pattern for the yellow horse (dress) and blue horse (bag).

KEY
YELLOW HORSE
1 and 3 – 0120 Delphinium
2 – 0943 Maize

BLUE HORSE
1 and 3 – 0120 Delphinium
2 – 0940 Hyacinth

Making the bag
(Finished size 6 × 7in (15 × 17·5cm)

6 From the remaining yellow fabric cut two pieces 9¼ × 6¾in (24 × 17cm). Transfer the horse motif onto the blue fabric and prepare with Bondaweb, as for the pinafore. Cut out the motif. Peel off the paper backing and iron the motif onto the yellow fabric 1½in (4cm) from the lower edge.

7 Work the embroidery as for the pinafore; make and attach the mane and tail.

8 Place front and back of bag together, right sides facing. Stitch across the bottom edge taking ½in (12mm) seam. Stitch the side seams for 6¼in (15.5cm) up from the lower edge, leave ½in (12mm) unstitched, then stitch remaining side seams.

9 Turn to the right side. Turn ¼in (6mm) on top edge to wrong side and baste. Fold hem to wrong side so that the folded edge lies just below the opening at the side seams. Baste, then stitch above and below the opening to make a casing for the cord.

10 Thread the cord through the casing, knot 2½in (6.5cm) from the raw ends. Remove basting stitches.

Peel away the backing fabric.

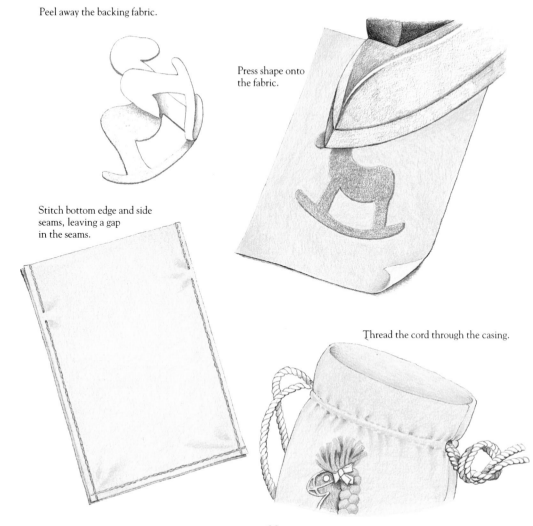

Press shape onto the fabric.

Stitch bottom edge and side seams, leaving a gap in the seams.

Thread the cord through the casing.

The rocking horse motif on the simple drawstring bag
makes a pretty, co-ordinated accessory for a little girl.
For a party look, why not trim the bag with a broderie
Anglaise frill?

Nursery friends

Bears together

This romantic bears picture will be everyone's favourite, from toddlers to newlyweds, and you may find you have a lot of requests for it. Luckily, long stitch pictures are quick and easy to work so hopefully no one will be disappointed.

Materials

18-count single thread canvas 10in (25cm) square

DMC soft cotton – 1 skein each of the following colours – salmon 2350, aqua 2599, brown 2610, pale yellow 2745, gold 2782, petrol blue 2924, dark aqua 2956, mid-aqua 2957, green 1101; 2 skeins of dark blue 2826

Tapestry needle

Round Flexi-frame 6in (15cm) diameter.

Preparation

1 Cover the edges of the canvas with masking tape to prevent fraying.

2 Place the canvas on top of the pattern on this page and trace the outline pattern with a waterproof pen.

3 Mount the canvas into the Flexi-frame. Alternatively, work the embroidery in the hand but cover the canvas edges with masking tape to prevent fraying.

Working the embroidery

4 Work the long satin stitches (see diagram), following the colours and key. Make sure stitches are kept firm and even, but not tight.

5 When working satin stitch on canvas, start by making a small backstitch on the line of the first stitch. This will be covered as the stitch is worked. Finish off by darning the thread and through the back of the stitches.

Making up

6 Place the canvas in the Flexi-frame if you have been working the canvas in your hands. Trim off the excess canvas, leaving enough to lace the edges.

7 Lace the canvas edges using strong thread and working from side to side.

8 Cut a circle of thin white card and glue to the back of the embroidery.

Work satin stitches of different lengths to fill the shape.

Lace canvas edges together using strong thread.

KEY
1 – White
2 – Pale yellow
3 – Salmon
4 – Aqua
5 – Mid-aqua
6 – Dark aqua
7 – Petrol blue
8 – Dark blue
9 – Gold
10 – Brown

Beach bears

This delightful picture would make a lovely gift for a young child or a new baby. The companion picture, Bears Together, is on pages 34–35. Both pictures are worked in soft cotton thread on canvas and put into a Flexi-frame afterwards.

Materials for the embroidery

10ins (25cm) square piece of 18-count white
  single thread canvas
DMC soft cotton – 1 skein of each of the
  following colours – 2350, 2436, 2472,
  2599, 2610, 2726, 2738, 2745, 2782,
  2828, 2938 and 1101
Tapestry needle
Round Flexi-frame 6in (15cm) diameter.

Preparation

1 Cover the edges of the canvas with
masking tape to prevent fraying.

2 Place the canvas on top of the pattern on
this page and trace the outline pattern with
a waterproof pen.

3 Mount the canvas into the Flexi-frame.

Alternatively, work the embroidery in the
hand.

Working the embroidery

4 Work the long satin stitches (see
diagram), following the colours and key.
Make sure stitches are kept firm and even,
but not tight.

5 When working satin stitch on canvas,
start off by first making a small backstitch on
the line of the first stitch. This will be
covered as the stitch is worked. Finish off by
darning the thread end through the back of
the stitching.

6 Work dark brown backstitches for Bears'
smiles, and for the boat's mast. Finish as for
the Bears' together picture.

Using Flexi-frames

These useful pieces of embroidery
equipment are designed so that your
finished embroidery can be slipped
easily between the two hoops for quick
and efficiency framing. The frame has a
small hanger on one side. If you prefer,
you can use your Flexi-frame as an
embroidery hoop also. Mounting canvas
into a Flexi-frame is described on page
34. Lacing threads are used to hold the
canvas neatly on the wrong side. For
embroidered fabric the technique is
different.
    Use the inner hoop to mark the
frame shape on the fabric (use
dressmakers' carbon pencil) centring
the design. Gather on the line, then
slip the fabric over the inner hoop.
Press the soft, hoop on top. Trim fabric
on wrong side. Glue paper or thin card
to cover.

KEY
1 – White   4 – Salmon   7 – Light blue   10 – Gold
2 – Pale yellow 5 – Green   8 – Light beige   11 – Light brown
3 – Dark yellow 6 – Aqua   9 – Dark beige   12 – Dark brown

3: LITTLE GIFTS

Smart Set

This pencil tidy and clip box are made from plastic canvas and knitting yarn and would make a useful gift for a budding scholar or an adult.

PENCIL TIDY

Materials
Finished size 5¼in (13cm) × 3¼in (8cm)
Plastic canvas, sheet 10½ × 13½in
    (26 × 34cm) with 7 holes to 1 in (2.5in)
Double knitting yarn in white, navy blue,
    royal blue and turquoise
Blunt-ended tapestry needle with
    a large eye.

Preparation
1 Using a ball-point pen and ruler, measure and mark four pieces for the sides, 5¼ × 3¼in (13 × 8cm) and a base piece 3¼in (8cm) square. (Mark the lines between the 'ribs'.)

2 Cut out the pieces, trimming projecting bits back to the main 'rib', being careful to cut up to it, not into it.

3 The pattern is the same on all four sides. Mark the pattern using ruler and ball-point pen.

Working the embroidery
4 Using a single strand of yarn work cross stitch over one intersection of threads each way. Follow the key for colours. Leave one hole unworked all round for joining pieces.

5 To form the box, place two long sides together, wrong side inward. Work the braided cross stitch in the navy blue yarn all along the edge. Repeat with the other sides, but before closing the two final edges, place the base in position and cross stitch all round before the last side is closed.

6 Finish with braided cross stitch all round the top using a longer than normal length of yarn so that you do not have to make a join. Follow the diagram on this page.

MATCHING BOX

Materials
6 pieces 2in (5cm) square of plastic canvas,
    7 holes to 1in (2.5cm)
Small amounts of hand knitting yarn from
    the box project
Small round bead.

Preparation
1 Cut and prepare the squares as before.

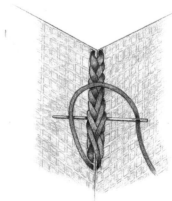

Braided stitch: Bring needle from back through first hole, go over edges and through fifth hole. Go over edges and through second hole, then go over edges and through the sixth hole.

Working the embroidery

2 Proceed in the same way as before.

3 Work the braided stitch on 3 sides of the lid before placing the unstitched edge to the matching unstitched edge on the top. Work the final braided edge allowing some ease so that it makes a flexible 'hinge'.

4 To fasten the box make a plait 2¹/₂in (7cm) long with 3 lengths of yarn, stitch to the underside of the lid to make a central loop hanging down to the right side.

5 Sew the bead to the front to correspond with the loop fastening. If you prefer, a ball button could be used.

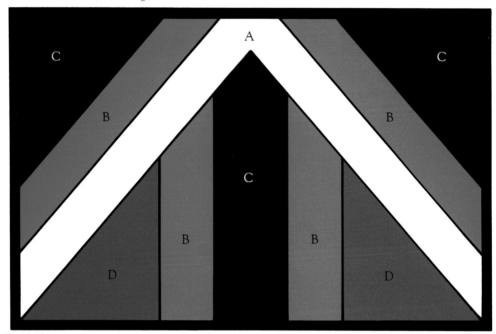

Pencil tidy

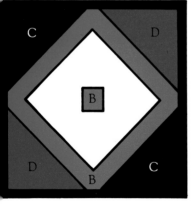

Small box

KEY
A – white
B – turquoise
C – navy blue
D – royal blue

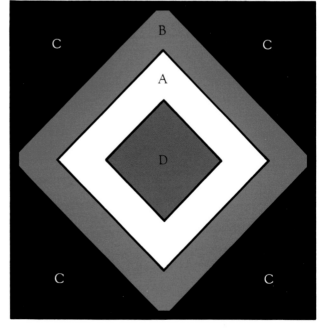

Sweet scents of summer!

Harvest nature's bounty and capture it in these pretty pot-pourri bags to remind you of summer. Dainty embroidery worked on fine broderie Anglaise makes these acceptable gifts for friends and families.

Materials
Finished sizes – pink bow 7 × 3³/₄in
   (18 × 9.5cm), blue roses and yellow
   flowers 7 × 2³/₄in (18 × 7cm)
White broderie Anglaise 14¹/₂ × 8in
   (37 × 20cm)
Thin polyester wadding, 14¹/₂in × 6in
   (37 × 15cm)
Dried lavender, ready-mixed pot-pourri
Double-faced satin ribbon ¹/₄in (6mm) wide
   in pink, blue and lemon, 17in (43cm)
   lengths
Anchor stranded cotton, in the following
   colours: **Pink bow:** pink 25, yellow 295,
   fuchsia 57, lilac 96, green 255 (small
   amounts); **Blue roses:** blue 161, pale blue
   158, yellow 295, lilac 96, green 280,
   violet 97; **Yellow flowers:** yellow 297,
   green 280, dark green 817
Small embroidery hoop (optional).

Preparation
1 Trace off and transfer the patterns on to
the fabric (work the embroidery before
cutting out).

Working the embroidery
2 Use two strands of embroidery thread
throughout. Work the embroidery following
the colours and stitches indicated on the
patterns. Darn ends in neatly on the wrong
side.

Making the bags
3 Cut out the bags with the embroidery
motifs centred. For the Pink bow sachet, cut
to 7 × 3³/₄in (18 × 9.5cm), for Blue roses
and Yellow flowers, cut to 7 × 2³/₄in
(18 × 7cm).

4 Turn and sew a narrow hem on the top
edge. Use tiny hemming stitches.

5 Fold right sides facing and stitch the long
edges taking a ¹/₄in (6mm) seam. Centre the
seam at the back, stitch across the bottom.
Turn to the right side.

6 Make a small wadding bag to fit inside, fill
with pot-pourri or lavender.

7 Push the wadding bag down inside the
sachet, tie a ribbon round the top.

Direct tracing
When fine, semi-transparent fabrics –
such as cotton lawn – are used for
embroidery, designs can be transferred
to the fabric by the direct tracing
method. Place the design over a direct
light source, such as a light box or a
window, with the fabric on top. Draw
over the lines with embroidery pencil.

Blue roses

Satin stitch

Prick stitch

Stem stitch

Bullion knots

Yellow flowers

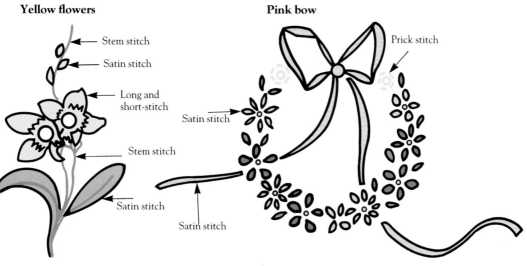

Stem stitch

Satin stitch

Long and short-stitch

Stem stitch

Satin stitch

Satin stitch

Pink bow

Prick stitch

Satin stitch

Satin stitch

Persian birds

These mythological birds, greeting the dawn, are embroidered in crewel wool on linen. The design is intended for a picture or wall hanging, but the components could be abstracted and repeated in several different arrangements for other types of furnishing.

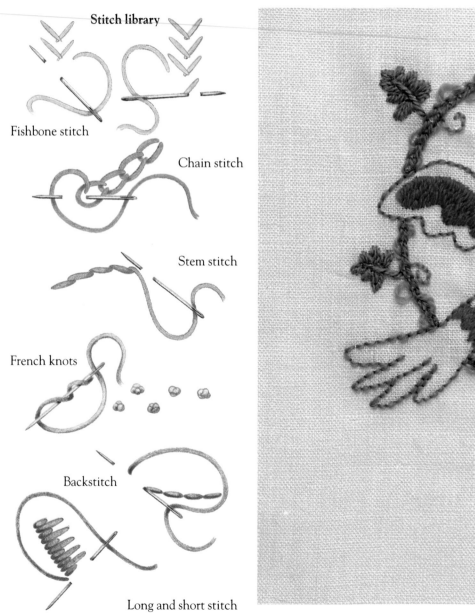

Stitch library

Fishbone stitch

Chain stitch

Stem stitch

French knots

Backstitch

Long and short stitch

Materials

Finished size of pattern 8 × 7in (20 × 18cm)
Fine linen 13 × 17in (33 × 43cm)
Paterna Persian yarn 1 skein each of the
    following colours: gold A733, lime A735,
    light sage A604, jade A552, rust D234,
    chocolate A482, pale chocolate A485,
    scarlet A952
Crewel needle
Embroidery frame.

Preparation

1 Trace the pattern on pages 46–47 and
transfer to the fabric.

Working the embroidery

2 Follow the pattern and key on page 46 for
the colours and stitches, using a single
strand of the embroidery yarn. Leave the
yellow vine until the end; this is worked by
threading the wool through the chain stitches.

Trace-off patterns for Persian birds

The Persian birds design is typical of
crewel embroidery and can be used to
decorate a variety of home furnishings.
It is ideally sized for a 14in (35cm)
cushion or for a picture. However, the
design could be separated bird motifs
which might be repeated horizontally or
vertically. For instance, motifs could be
worked across a bolster or several birds
could be worked down a door curtain.
Other techniques: You can also use the
design for surface embroidery –
experiment with random-dyed stranded
embroidery threads, perhaps mixed with
metallic yarns. By copying the design
onto squared paper, you could use it for
cross stitch embroidery or for
canvaswork.

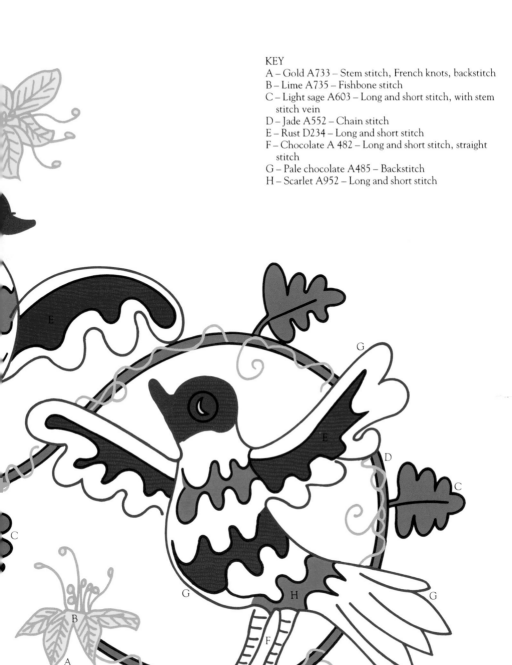

KEY
A – Gold A733 – Stem stitch, French knots, backstitch
B – Lime A735 – Fishbone stitch
C – Light sage A603 – Long and short stitch, with stem stitch vein
D – Jade A552 – Chain stitch
E – Rust D234 – Long and short stitch
F – Chocolate A 482 – Long and short stitch, straight stitch
G – Pale chocolate A485 – Backstitch
H – Scarlet A952 – Long and short stitch

Trace the pattern, joining where indicated with arrows.

Practical pair

The matching needlecase and wrist pincushion will be welcomed by a dedicated sewer. Both items are decorated with chain stitches.

Materials

For the needlecase 3½ × 6½in
  (9 × 16.5cm), and a wrist pincushion
  2½in (6cm) square)
Blue firmly woven fabric 12½ × 7½in
  (32 × 19cm)
Red felt 6in (15cm) square
Red ribbon 10in (25cm) long, ½in (12mm)
  wide
Coton perle no 5, 1 skein each of scarlet 350
  and red 817
Small amount of no 20 white crochet cotton
Blue and red sewing threads
Velcro self-fastening tape, 1in (2.5cm) long
Polyester toy filling.

NEEDLECASE

Preparation

1 From the blue fabric cut two pieces
4½ × 7½in (11.5 × 19cm). Trace and
transfer the pattern, positioning it in the
centre.

2 Using chain stitch throughout, work the
outline first in red 817. Work the inner line
in scarlet 350.

3 Place the two pieces of fabric together
with the embroidery on the inside and stitch
a ¼in (6mm) seam on two long sides and
one short side. Clip the corners, turn to the
right side. Turn in the open edges and close
with small stitches.

4 Cut the felt in half. Place centrally on the
inside of the needle case and stitch the felt
pages to the spine using blue thread and
small stitches.

5 Finish the edges of the needlecase with
one strand of red perle couched in place with
blue thread.

PINCUSHION

Preparation

6 From the remaining fabric cut a piece
4 × 7½in (10 × 19cm). Trace the circular
design and transfer onto the top half of the
piece, centring it.

Working the embroidery

7 Using chain stitch throughout, work the
outline first in red 817. Work the inner line
in scarlet 350.

8 Finish the embroidery with the white
crochet cotton for the outer line and the
small, infill areas.

Making the pincushion

9 Cut and trim the fabric so that you have
two pieces 3½in (9cm) square.

10 Put the two pieces together with the
embroidery facing inwards and sew together
with a ½in (12mm) seam on three sides.
Clip into the corners and trim off
diagonally. Turn to the right side.

11 Stuff the cushion firmly, turn the edges
of the open end in ½in (12mm), close with
small stitches.

Finishing

12 Turn one end of the ribbon under ¾in
(18mm) and oversew one piece of the
Velcro to it.

13 Fit the ribbon to the wrist to determine
where the other piece of Velcro goes. Fold
under the excess fabric, sew on the Velcro.

14 Centre the ribbon on the back of the
pincushion and sew with small stitches to
attach it firmly.

Country cottage

This charming cottage design with roses round the door is worked in cross stitch and French knots with backstitch details.

KEY

⊡ – Pale blue	◙ – Dark brown	△ – White	▲ – Dark green	⫼ – Pale pink
◈ – Beige	✦ – Deep pink	⊞ – Bright green	✕ – Grey	◉ – Dark beige
◨ – Mink brown	◩ – Light green	◼ – Mid-green		

Materials

Aida 18-count embroidery fabric 8in (20cm) square

Green Flexi-frame 5in/12.5cm diameter

DMC stranded cotton in the following colours (very small amounts are needed) pale blue 794, mink brown 642, dark beige 433, dark green 895, beige 842, deep pink 350, pale pink 605, dark brown 840, light green 471, grey 931, bright green 906, mid-green 3053, white 3689

Crewel needle.

Preparation

1 Work machine stitch or oversew round the fabric edges to prevent fraying.

2 Measure and mark the middle of the fabric vertically and horizontally with lines of basting stitches.

3 Place the fabric in the embroidery frame and pull evenly all round until the fabric is smooth and taut.

Working the embroidery

4 The chart for the design shows one square for each cross stitch which is worked over a 2 thread intersection using 3 strands together. The middle of the chart is indicated with arrows on the edges to correspond with the basting lines.

5 Begin embroidery in the middle of the design following the colour key symbols.

6 Using backstitch throughout and with 2 strands of thread, work the window outlines in mink brown, underline the roofs in dark brown, work rose stems in dark pink.

7 French knot roses are worked on top of the finished embroidery. Lace the fabric on card before framing.

It's a gift

Little Christmas tree decorations like these boots are just big enough to take small gifts – such as lipstick, a small bottle of perfume, coins, etc. Use felt and scraps of lace or an attractive Christmas print fabric.

Materials
(for red and green boots)
Felt 4in (10cm) square in red and green
Scraps of dark green felt
Small amounts of coton perle in blue, white and pale green
Gold thread
Gold beads
Small length of narrow red ribbon

Preparation
1 Trace off and transfer the boot shape twice to fit in to each square of felt. Cut out with sharp scissors.

2 Trace off and transfer the small ivy leaves to the dark green felt and cut out.

3 Mark the lines of embroidery on the red boot and the position of the ivy leaves and the trails on one side of the green boot.

Working the embroidery
4 On the red boot, work the detached chain stitches along the top in white, with French knots in blue. Work the detached chain stitches along the bottom edge of the boot in blue, with gold beads centred on each. Work running stitches in the zig-zag pattern in blue, then lace gold thread through each stitch. Work small, double cross stiches in white above and below the zig-zag line. Blanket-stitch the top edges in blue. Work both sides of the boot in the same way.

5 On the green boot, place the ivy shapes in position and pin. Using pale green coton perle work stem stitch for the trails. Attach the leaves to the boot with long straight stitches to make the veins. Oversew a length of red ribbon just below the top edge. Work both sides of the boot in the same way.

Making up the boots
6 Baste the boot sides together, right side out. Machine-stitch close to the edge (or work buttonhole stitch).

7 Stitch a short length of gold thread at the back seam for a hanger.

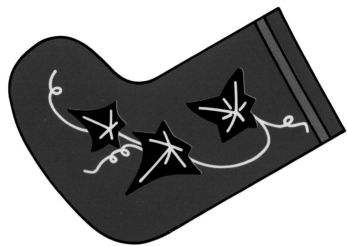

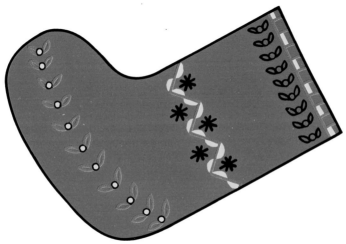

Special greetings

Both designs, the bells and the festive tree, use the misty effect of a top layer of organza to soften the strong colour of the felt beneath.

CHRISTMAS TREE

Materials

Green felt 3³/₄in (9.5cm) square
Pale green organza 3³/₄in (9.5cm) square
Twilleys Goldfingering crochet thread (or thick metallic embroidery thread)
13 gold beads ¹/₈th in (3mm) diameter
Spray mount glue (or general purpose glue)
Card with pre-cut window, to take finished image 3³/₄in (9.5cm).

Preparation

1 Trace the tree shape and transfer onto thin card. Cut out and use as a template to cut the shape from green felt.

2 Spray glue on the shape and place onto the middle of the pale green organza.

3 Place the organza down with the green felt shape underneath and transfer the lines for the gold stitching onto the top of the organza.

Working the embroidery

4 Work backstitch on the lines with the gold thread. Make a double cross stitch at the top of the tree for the star. Work straight stitches across for the tub.

5 Sew on the gold beads.

6 Spread glue round the window of the card on the inside and place the embroidery in position. Press firmly and leave to dry, then glue the return fold around the embroidery and press firmly.

Materials needed (for the bells)

Fuschia pink felt 3³/₄in (9.5cm) square
Pale pink organza 3³/₄in (9.5cm) square
Silver thread Mez Ophir No 0301
Small length of white parcel ribbon
1 small glass bead
Pre-cut card with a window to take work
3³/₄in (9.5cm).

Preparation

1 Trace the bells' shape and transfer to thin card. Cut out and use as a template to cut the shape from pink felt. Spray glue on the shape and place down onto the middle of the pink organza. Leave to dry.

2 Turn the organza over and transfer the pattern lines of the bells onto it.

Working the embroidery

3 Work backstitch neatly on the lines of the bells, leaving the lower edges of the main bell until last. Use a neat, close, chain stitch to embroider this line. Work small straight stitches for the clapper and sew the glass bead at the bottom.

Making up

Follow the instructions for the first card. The reversed shadow effect using organza can be utilized to make many different cards from these two designs. You could also use chiffon or voile as the top layer. Try different combinations using other coloured felts underneath.

> These motifs are ideal for making soft Christmas tree decorations. Cut the shapes from doubled felt and embroider the design lines, adding beads and sequins. Sew the two shapes together, stuffing them lightly with polyester wadding. Attach a gold thread hanger.

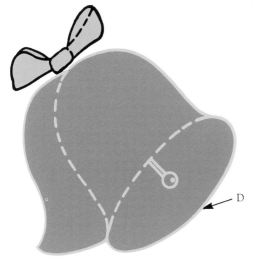

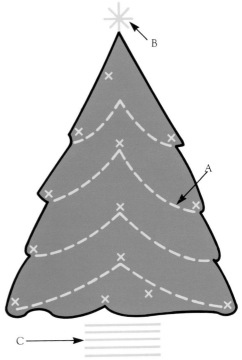

KEY
A – Backstitch
B – Double cross stitch
C – Straight stitch
D – Chain stitch

Christmas cameo

Embroider this pretty little cameo to take pride of place in your Christmas decorations. It would also make an acceptable present for someone who appreciates fine handwork.

Materials

Zweigart fabric 'Salamanca' in cream, 6in (16cm) square
DMC stranded cotton – 1 skein each of red 57, yellow 94, pink 743, white and random-dyed almond green
Crewel needle
Red Flexi-frame 3in (7.5cm) diameter
Thin card

Preparation

1 Trace the pattern and transfer to the fabric.

2 Place the fabric in the Flexi-frame (if desired).

Working the embroidery

3 Using two strands of thread together work the embroidery following the key for colours and stitches.

Making up

4 Remove the work from the frame and lightly press on the back.

5 Using the frame as a guide, pencil a circle on card. Cut out and place on wrong side of the fabric, centring the design.

6 Lightly pencil round. Work basting stitches round the circle $1/4$in (6mm) outside the line. Draw up to fit embroidery over the card circle. Trim all round. Finish thread end with back stitches.

7 Put the mounted embroidery back in the Flexi-frame.

8 Cut a circle of paper and glue to the back of the embroidery if desired, but use a white PVC adhesive sparingly. (This technique is illustrated on page 37.)

KEY
1 Pink, red – Long and short stitch
2 Yellow – Long and short stitch
3 Almond green – Long and short stitch
4 Red – Long and short stitch
5 Pink – Long and short stitch
6 2 Almond, 1 white thread – French knots
7 White – French knots

4: HOMEMAKERS

Lilies on linen

Beautiful embroidered linens make every mealtime a special event. The quantities of fabric and threads given here are for one place mat and a matching napkin.

Materials

Finished sizes: place mat 16½ × 11in (42 × 28cm), napkin 16¼in (41cm) square.

White linen (or ready-made place mat) 17 × 11½in (43 × 29.5cm)

Red linen (or good-quality cotton fabric) 16¾in (43cm) square

DMC stranded embroidery cotton, 1 skein each of scarlet 321, red 304, burgundy 815, gold 972, yellow 973, green 471, white and ecru

Embroidery hoop

Red sewing thread.

PLACEMAT

Preparation

1 Trace the lily pattern and transfer twice to the white place mat fabric, one motif above the other (see picture). The small bud on the right hand side should be 1in (2.5cm) in from the edge.

Working the embroidery

2 Place the fabric in the embroidery hoop and work the design, following the key for stitches and colours. Use 3 strands of embroidery cotton throughout.

3 When embroidery is completed, darn in loose ends on the wrong side and lightly press on the wrong side.

4 Trace the scalloped-edged corner and transfer to the upper left-hand corner of the fabric, about ½in (12mm) from the edge. Move the tracing to complete scallops all round the place mat.

5 Work a close, machine-satin stitch on the scallops.

6 Cut the excess fabric away, close to the stitching, using a small, sharp pair of embroidery scissors.

NAPKIN

Preparation
Transfer the lily pattern without the left hand bud (see photograph, page 60). Position the motif on the bottom, left hand corner. Work the design as for the place mat, and finish in the same way.

When working machine satin stitch, place a piece of tissue paper between the fabric and the machine's plate. The paper is torn away after the embroidery has been worked. If you prefer a hand finish on your linens, small, close buttonhole stitch can be worked on the scallops. Trim the excess fabric away afterwards using embroidery scissors.

A – Scarlet
B – Red
C – Burgundy
D – Gold
E – Yellow
F – Green

Trace-off pattern for the
lily motif and part of the scalloped edge.
Move the tracing when transferring
to obtain the complete edge

Flower Fresh

Here is a novel way of keeping the air sweet. A block of air freshener (or a pot-pourri sachet) is placed in the pocket behind the basket of felt flowers. Hung in a room it provides a discreet fragrance.

Materials
Beige felt, 8in (20cm) square
Leaf green, red felt 6in (15cm) square
White felt 4in (10cm) square
Anchor stranded cotton in black, beige, red
   and pale green
Adhesive (PVA or similar)
Scrap of thin card (to fit the back pocket
   section)
Crewel needle.

Preparation
1 Trace the pattern pieces, on this page and overleaf, onto paper and cut out.

2 Pin patterns to the relevant coloured felt. Cut out with sharp scissors. Cut two basket pieces from beige felt, then trim one piece along broken line (see pattern) for the pocket.

Making the holder
3 Place back and pocket pieces together with the rounded end matching and prick stitch together on the curved edge.

4 Using three strands of beige cotton work four rows of chain stitch down the basket front (see picture). Glue the leaf shape in place and leave to dry.

5 Embroider the felt flowers: outline the poppy petals in red stem stitch, using 2 strands. Work black stamens in stem stitch using 6 strands, finishing with a French Knot at the ends. Add a few pale green satin stitches to the poppy bud using 2 strands. Work green French Knots in the middle of the daisies. Detail the daisy buds with pale green stem stitch, using 2 strands.

6 Glue the flowers in position on the green felt leaf, overlapping the largest poppy on the half-opened poppy.

7 On the centre back make a buttonhole-stitched hanging loop.

8 Cut a piece of thin card to insert into the pocket to stiffen it.

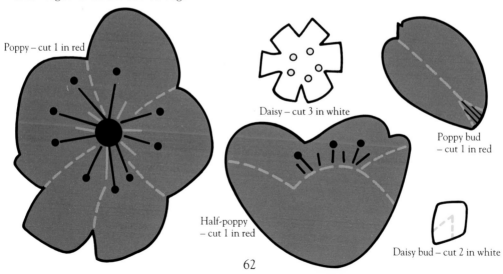

Poppy – cut 1 in red

Daisy – cut 3 in white

Poppy bud – cut 1 in red

Half-poppy – cut 1 in red

Daisy bud – cut 2 in white

62

Make a thread loop on the back of the holder with buttonhole stitches over 5 or 6 threads

The motif could also be used for surface embroidery. Trace the components (except the basket) on a sheet of paper, arranging them as shown in the picture. Transfer to fabric. Work poppies in long and short stitch, leaves in satin stitch, daisies in straight stitches. Use stranded cotton or coton perle.

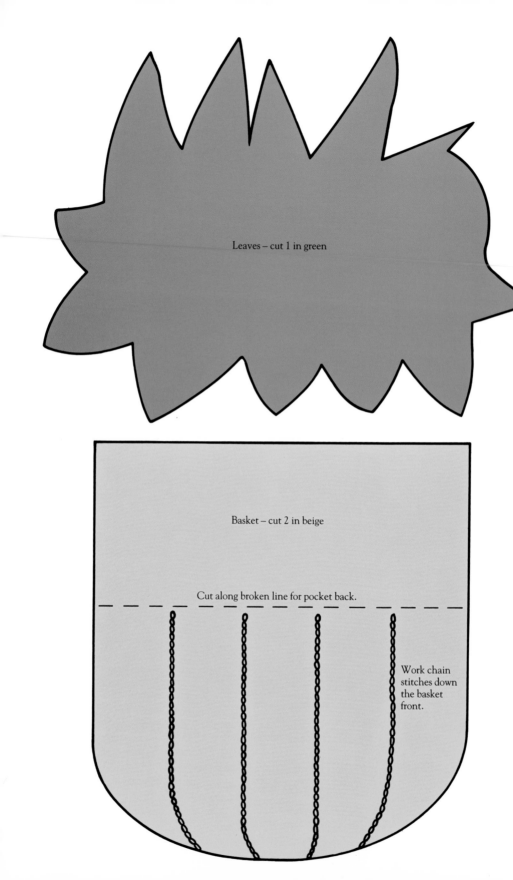

Leaves – cut 1 in green

Basket – cut 2 in beige

Cut along broken line for pocket back.

Work chain
stitches down
the basket
front.

Ribbon bouquet

The embroidery on this cushion is worked with tubular hand knitting yarn or 'knitting ribbon'. If this is not available you can use satin ribbon instead. The stitches are bold to use the yarn to its best advantage.

Put the knotted strands over a door handle,
insert a pencil in the other end and twist clockwise

Materials
Finished size of motif 7 × 7¹/₂in
   (18 × 19.5cm)
2 pieces of evenly-woven fabric 14¹/₂in
   (37cm) square
1 ball each of yellow and white knitting
   ribbon
A large-eyed blunt-ended darning needle.

Preparation
1 Trace the outlines of the flowers and
transfer to the fabric.

Working the embroidery
2 One strand of the knitting ribbon is used
throughout the embroidery. Work the large
yellow flower petals in detached chain
stitch, and the tiny white flowers in small
straight stitches. Work French knots in
white or yellow yarn in the positions shown.

3 The raised centres of some of the large
flowers are made by embroidering 3 or 4 long
stitches horizontally across the centres and
then weaving in and out vertically.

4 Make the stems by taking long, loose
stitches down from under the flowers. Fasten
off the ends on the wrong side then work
three or four horizontal stitches 1in (2.5cm)
from the stem ends to pull them together.
Fasten off yarn ends on the back.

5 Make up as described for the Rosebud
cushion on page 68.

Finishing
6 To make the plaited ribbon edge, cut 3
yellow and 3 white 4yd (4.5m) lengths.

Ribbon bouquet

Trace this design, joining the two sections where
indicated with arrows.

Knot the strands together at each end, put
one end over a doorknob and slip a pencil in
the other end. Turn the pencil clockwise
until the strands are tightly twisted.

7 Remove from the handle and fold the
strands in half and they will twist together.
Pull gently to even out the twists. Knot both
ends again.

8 Pin the twisted cord round the cushion,
starting and ending at a corner. Open the
seams a little and tuck the ends down inside.
Sew the plait along the seam line using
matching thread.

This is an ideal design for working in surface embroidery, using either stranded threads or pearl cotton. Work the flower centres in massed French knots, with the petals in satin stitch. Straight stitches and French knots can be used for the other flowers, with the stems in stem stitch. If the design were enlarged a little, crewel wools could also be used, working on embroidery linen.

Rosebuds

Bullion knots and detached chain stitches are used to form the little rosebuds that decorate this cushion. Once you have mastered the technique you'll find dozens of uses for them, from babies' and children's clothes to pretty fashion accessories.

Materials

Finished size $15^{1}/_{2} \times 15^{1}/_{2}$in ($39 \times 39$cm)
Two pieces of glazed cotton fabric each
$16^{1}/_{2} \times 16^{1}/_{2}$in ($42 \times 42$cm)
Thin, washable, wadding 16in (40cm)
square
Muslin 16in (40cm) square
Zip fastener 13in (33cm) long to match
fabric
Matching sewing thread
DMC stranded cotton, 1 skein each in the
following colours: blue-grey 926, pink
605, bright pink 956
Milwards no 5 crewel needle.

Preparation

1 Sandwich the wadding between the muslin and one piece of the glazed cotton. Pin together, baste from side to side and from top to bottom and then from corner to corner.

2 Measure and mark the lines shown on the quilting pattern, using an embroidery pencil. Machine-stitch along the lines using a medium-to-large stitch, or by hand using running stitches or backstitch. Work the inner, diamond pattern first, then the outer square and the corners.

Working the embroidery

3 Measure and mark the centres of the twelve diamond shapes. With three strands of bright pink 956 in the needle, work seven bullion knots for the centres of the roses, curving them as you work so that they enfold each other, like petals. Make five more bullion knot petals around the centre using three strands of pink 605.

4 With two strands of blue-grey 926, work elongated detached chain stitches for the leaves.

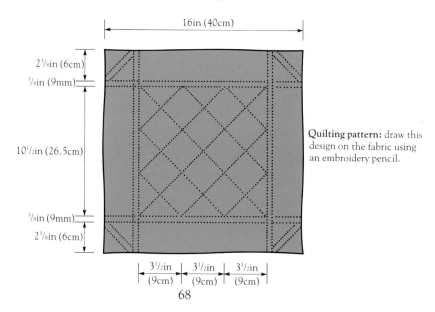

16in (40cm)

$2^{3}/_{8}$in (6cm)

$^{3}/_{8}$in (9mm)

$10^{1}/_{2}$in (26.5cm)

$^{3}/_{8}$in (9mm)

$2^{3}/_{8}$in (6cm)

$3^{1}/_{2}$in (9cm) $3^{1}/_{2}$in (9cm) $3^{1}/_{2}$in (9cm)

Quilting pattern: draw this design on the fabric using an embroidery pencil.

Making up the cushion

5 Place the two embroidered cushion fronts to the cotton back, right sides facing. Pin, baste, stitch on three sides taking ³/₈in (9mm) seams. Clip into the corners to ease the seam and turn to right side out. Centre the zip fastener on the open seam, pin and stitch. On the wrong side of work, stitch the remaining seam at the zipper ends. Remove all basting stitches.

Bring the thread through at A and insert at B.

Twist the thread 5 or 6 times round the needle.

Reinsert the needle at B and bring out again ready for the next bullion knot.

Personal touches

Embroidered towels are quite costly to buy but they are so easy and inexpensive to make yourself. The three designs shown here are worked in simple stitches, and with very little adaptation, can be personalized with initials or a name.

CAMELLIA

Materials
Towel
Matching sewing thread
White cotton fabric 8in (20cm) square
DMC stranded embroidery cotton, 1 skein each of the following colours: pink 818, blue 3752 and 3761, random-dyed blue 67
Embroidery hoop.

Preparation
1 Trace, then transfer, the pattern to the centre of the fabric (place it slightly above the centre if you want to work a name or initials below).

2 Place the fabric in the embroidery hoop.

Working the embroidery
3 Work the embroidery using three strands of embroidery thread throughout. Work the petal outlines in buttonhole stitch, using random-dyed blue. Work the veins on the petals in running stitch, using blue 3761. Work the stamens in satin stitch, using pink 818. Work the leaves in satin stitch using blue 3752.

4 If a name is being added, write the name below the finished embroidery, using a pale blue embroidery pencil, then embroider in small stem stitches, using two strands of embroidery thread.

5 On the back of the embroidery make a circle 6³/₄in (17cm) diameter, centrally placed on the embroidery. Cut out and baste in position on the towel.

6 Thread the matching thread in the sewing machine. Work around the circle with a close zig-zag satin stitch. Fasten off the threads on the back.
You could use these designs as small pictures to match the towels in your bathroom, and put them onto your towelling gown for a complete set.

HAREBELLS

Materials
Towel
Blue polyester cotton fabric 5¹/₂in (14cm) square
Matching sewing thread
DMC stranded cotton in the following colours: green 563, blue 799, dark blue 796, dark emerald 933
Embroidery hoop.

Preparation
1 Trace, then transfer, the pattern to the centre of the fabric (place it slightly above centre if you want to add a name below).

2 Place the fabric in the embroidery hoop.

Both of the designs on pages 72–73 would be ideal for appliqué, using satin fabrics. Trace the outlines and transfer to the fabric. Work any details at this stage.
  Work round the outlines with narrow machine satin stitch, then cut out ¹/₈in (3mm) from the stitching. Baste to the towel, then work wider machine satin stitch over the edges.

Working the embroidery

3 Use three strands of embroidery thread throughout. Work the petals in satin stitch using blue 799 with the back petals in dark blue 796. Work the calyx in satin stitch using green 563. Work the stems in stem stitch in green 563 and the leaves in satin stitch using emerald 933. Outline the leaves and work the veins in green 563.

4 Remove the fabric from the hoop. Draw a circle 4in (10cm) diameter on the back of the work. Cut out and baste in position on the towel.

5 Using matching sewing thread in the sewing machine, work a close zig-zag satin stitch edge round the edge of the circle.

DIAMOND EYELETS

Materials

Small hand towel (with an inset border for counted thread embroidery)
Coton perle no 5 in the following colours: light blue 3325, blue 826
Tapestry needle.

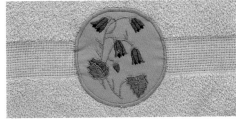

Preparation
1 Measure and mark the centre of the towel border both vertically and horizontally.

Working the embroidery
2 The long, centre stitch of the upper and lower diamonds meet at the mid-point of the border. Count 4 thread groups from the top centre edge (see diagram) and, bringing the thread through work the first stitch over 5 thread groups, using dark blue. From the centre hole, work stitches radiating round the centre point (see diagram).

3 The first stitch of the lower diamond is in the same hole of the lowest point of the first diamond. Work in the same way.

4 Place the side diamonds, one group of threads from either side, still using dark blue.

5 Change to pale blue and work 2 diamonds either side of the central dark blue design, one group of threads between them.

Names and initials
Towels can also be personalised by working names or initials in machine-satin stitch. Draw the letters on tissue paper first, then transfer to the towel using the basting thread method. Tear away the paper. Work a narrow satin stitch, then go over the lines with a wider stitch.

Seeing Stars

Decorate this useful bag with a shower of stars. Simple darning stitches are worked using the spots as a grid. It is the smart answer to keeping gloves and scarves together on a coat hanger or it can also be used for holding washday clothes pins.

Materials

2 pieces of spotted fabric 17 × 11in
  (43 × 28cm)
Small coat, or skirt, hanger 10in (25cm)
  wide with a bar
DMC coton perle no 5 in the following
  colours: gold 972, yellow 444 and white
Sewing thread to match the fabric.

Preparation

1 Stitch a ¹/₂in (12mm) hem on one short edge of both pieces. On one piece, turn the hem a further 4¹/₂in (11cm) to the inside. Machine-stitch a line of close satin stitch along the top edge. (This is to strengthen the edge as it will get a lot of wear.)

Working the embroidery

2 On the same side that has the satin stitch edge, work the embroidery, using the spots as a grid.

3 When finishing thread, darn into the embroidery on the back of the work.

Making up the bag

4 Place the two pieces of fabric right sides together and matching raw edges so that the back projects above the embroidered front. Stitch around three sides. Turn right side out.

5 Place the hanger on the top edge of the bag back and fold the extra fabric over it. Pin and baste in place. Sew close to the bar of the hanger with firm neat backstitches.

> Pattern darning is very quick and easy to work, but always make sure that the stitches are evenly made or the finished work will look puckered.

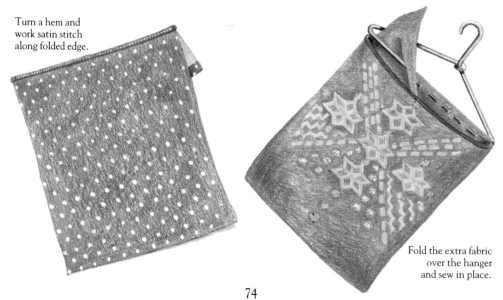

Turn a hem and work satin stitch along folded edge.

Fold the extra fabric over the hanger and sew in place.

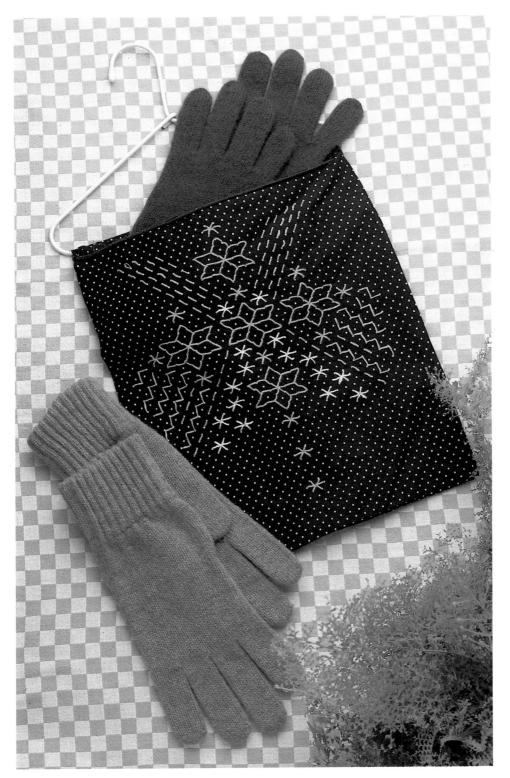

Curtain Up

When you are making cushions for a room scheme, use some of the fabric to make matching curtain ties. For a special decorative touch, hand-quilt the motifs and embellish your embroidery with additional decorative stitches.

Materials

Dressmakers' squared pattern paper, with
  1sq = 1in (2.5cm).
Printed, glazed cotton 30 × 5in
  (76 × 12.5cm)
Light-weight polyester wadding to
  the same size
Thin cotton or muslin
DMC stranded embroidery cotton, 1 skein
  each of the following colours: olive 3768,
  rose 3712, fuchsia 3607
Narrow furnishing cord, 2½yd (2.20m)
Crewel needle no 5
Two 1in (2.5cm) diameter rings

Preparation

1 From the graph, draw a pattern on squared paper. Cut the shape out. Extend the straight end if required.

2 Use the pattern to cut out from doubled printed cotton, adding ½in (12mm) all round. Cut the same shape in wadding and backing.

3 Place the printed fabric on the wadding and then place the backing underneath. Pin and baste all round.

4 Work larger shapes first. Using three strands of embroidery thread, work running stitches round the main shapes. When working, take the needle up and down vertically through the fabric.

5 Highlight and emphasize parts of the design with stitches such as French knots. Use them singly or in a massed effect.

Making up the tie

6 Machine-stitch all round leaving a 5in (12.5cm) gap in the seam. Clip into curves and turn to the right side. Turn in the open edge and sew up the opening.

7 Sew on the edging cord using very tiny stitches and a closely matching thread. Sew rings on the curtain tie ends.

Curtain tie Cut 1 each in fabric, wadding, backing.

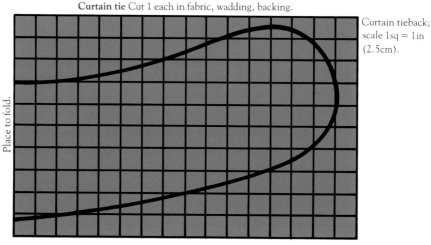

Curtain tieback; scale 1sq = 1in (2.5cm).

Place to fold.

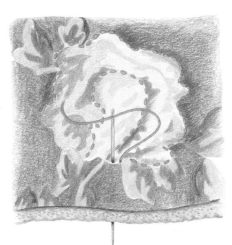

Work running stitches round the main shapes.

Sew on the edging cord with small stitches.

Daisy chains

Keep your expensive delicate tights or stockings in this soft broderie bag and you will know that they are safe from snags. The embroidery is easily worked, using only three stitches in soft pastel colours.

Materials needed

Finished size of bag $9\frac{1}{4} \times 10\frac{1}{2}$in
  (24×27cm)
White self edged Broderie Anglaise
  26×20in (66×51cm)
Polyester wadding 21×9in (54×23cm)
DMC stranded embroidery thread 1 skein
  each of the following colours: pink 818,
  turquoise 966, pale lilac 341, lilac 340
Needle
Tracing paper and pencil
Dressmakers' carbon paper.

Preparation

1 Lay the fabric out and decide where you are going to place the embroidery motif. It is best worked on a fairly unadorned area, keeping the heavier worked part for the top flap. The example here had the embroidery placed about $5\frac{1}{2}$in (14cm) down from the top front edge. Trace off and transfer the motif in your chosen position.

2 Work the embroidery with 3 strands throughout.

3 Fold the fabric in half with the embroidery inside, pin and stitch a seam $\frac{1}{2}$in (12mm) on the cut sides, leaving the decorative flap end unstitched.

KEY:
A – Pink 818 – satin stitch
B – Turquoise 966 – detached chain
C – Pale lilac 341, lilac 340 – detached chain
  with satin stitch centres.

Fold the fabric in half with the embroidery inside.

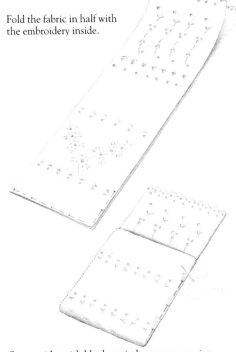

4 Turn to the right side and press. Slide the wadding inside the bag leaving the flap unstuffed.

5 Fold up the sides and pin together near to the edge. Work neat blanket stitch with white sewing cotton to close the sides.

6 Pin the open flap end along the borders and stitch together with small running stitches as invisibly as possible.

Sew up sides with blanket stitches or over-sewing.

5: FASHION EXTRAS

Edelweiss

This light-weight, pure wool shawl will be warm and comfortable in cooler weather. The colour scheme has been restrained to a range of wintry shades – brown, grey-green, pale lime and white and grey – to enhance the elegance of this luxurious accessory.

Materials
Ready made shawl or a piece of light-weight
  wool fabric approximately 36in (91cm)
  square
DMC Medici wool embroidery yarn,
  1 skein each of the following colours:
  8505 brown, 8204 light charcoal, 8211
  pale grey, 8509 grey green, 8421 lime
  green, 2 skeins of white
Embroidery transfer pencil
Tapestry needle no 24
Embroidery hoop

Preparation
1 Trace the pattern. Turn the paper over
and go over the outlines with an embroidery
transfer pencil. (The point must be very
sharp and the line on the paper must be as
finely drawn as possible.) Shake the paper to
make sure that no loose scraps of the transfer
pencil are left on the surface.

2 Place a soft, folded pad of fabric under the
corner of the shawl. Pin the pattern onto the
fabric, transfer-pencilled side down. With a
hot iron go over the surface of the pattern to
transfer it to the fabric. (You will see why
the line needed to be fine – the dye-loaded
line spreads under the hot iron.) Remove
the paper pattern and place the shawl corner
in the embroidery hoop.

Note: Remember to position the motif a
short distance in from the edges if a fringe is
desired.

Working the embroidery
3 Only two stitches are used in the design,
long and short satin stitch and French knots,
and these are worked with two single strands

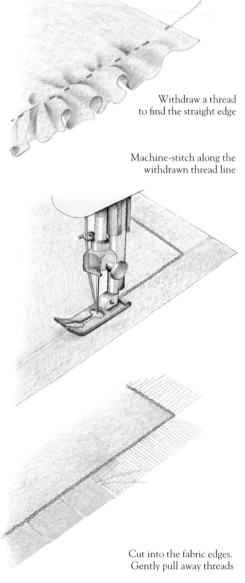

Withdraw a thread
to find the straight edge

Machine-stitch along the
withdrawn thread line

Cut into the fabric edges.
Gently pull away threads

of the embroidery wool. Edelweiss flowers and leaves have a rough, furry texture and the stitches should reflect this. Keep the long and short stitches a little uneven. Work the design following the pattern and key below for the colours and stitches.

4 When the embroidery is completed, remove the fabric from the hoop and lightly press the wrong side. Finish by turning a narrow hem and machine-stitching a hemming, or pull a fringe.

Fringing: Cut the fabric accurately square by drawing a thread all round and then cutting on this line. Measure 1¼in (3cm) in from the edges all round and withdraw a thread on all four sides. Set the sewing machine to a narrow zigzag stitch and stitch along the thread line. Cut into the raw edges at intervals, almost up to the stitching. Gently pull away the threads to leave the fringe.

For a quick embroidery effect, trace the edelweiss design on white fabric and colour in with fabric painting crayons. Make the colours permanent, following the manufacturer's instructions. Baste the fabric to thin wadding, then back with cotton lawn. Work small back-stitches round all the design lines, matching threads to the crayoned colours. This would make an ideal cushion cover.

KEY
A – 8505 brown
B – 8204 light charcoal
C – 8211 pale grey
D – 8509 grey green
E – 8421 lime green
F – white

Bunch of ribbons

This design was taken from a Japanese kimono and the simple lines translate well into chain stitches and a limited palette of colours. You will find many uses for this pretty motif – for fashion clothes and accessories as well as for decorative items in the home.

Materials

DMC stranded cotton, 1 skein each in the
following colours: deep sky blue 798,
bright blue 995, Duck-egg blue 747, mid-
blue 322, grey-blue 826, pale, sky blue
519
Crewel needle.

Preparation

1 Trace the motif from the picture and
transfer to the fabric in the desired position.
(To get a good imprint, place a piece of card
underneath the area before transferring).
Remove the pattern, trace over any faint
lines using a dressmakers' chalk pencil.

Note: If the fabric has a rough texture you
may need to work basting stitches over the
chalk lines to strengthen the image.

Working the embroidery

2 Following the key for colours and using
chain stitches throughout, work the
embroidery with 3 strands of thread in the
needle.

3 The stripes and individual chain stitches
are worked on top of the completed chain
stitch areas (see picture).

Try this motif in beadwork. Trace the
design onto fabric backed with
lightweight iron-on interfacing. Sew on
beads, either individually or in
quantities of 5 or 6, slipping beads onto
the needle, then passing the needle into
the fabric.

KEY
A – Deep, sky blue 798
B – Bright blue 995
C – Mid-blue 322
D – Grey-blue 826
E – Duck-egg blue 747 (for stripes)
F – Sky blue 519 (for spots)

Sweet raspberries

This neat little clutch bag will be very useful for both day and evening functions. The pattern is worked in red and navy but it could be worked in colours to suit your own wardrobe.

Materials needed

(Finished size 9 × 5¹⁄₂in (23 × 14cm)
DMC stranded cotton – red 321, navy 321 × 2 skeins
Natural linen 20 × 11in (51 × 28cm)
Pelmet Vilene 9 × 15¹⁄₂in (23 × 39cm)
Plain fabric for lining 10 × 16¹⁄₂in (25 × 42cm)
Needle
Embroidery hoop
Navy and natural sewing thread

Preparation

1 Press the linen flat with a hot iron, then measure and mark a rectangle 9 × 15¹⁄₂ (23 × 39cm). Mark the first third where the embroidery will be worked: this is an area 5¹⁄₂ × 9in (14in × 23cm). Trace off and transfer the pattern to the small marked area. Place the fabric in the embroidery hoop.

Working the embroidery

2 Work the raspberries with 3 strands of red stranded cotton. Make the stitches very close to each other and very firm; this will give them a slightly raised effect.

3 The leaves and border dots are worked with three strands of navy thread in satin stitch. Very close tight stem stitch with two strands is used for the stems.

To make up the bag

4 Press the embroidery lightly on the back and iron the lining fabric flat.

5 Place the embroidery face down on the table and place the pelmet Vilene onto it, make sure that it is central. Pin and tack the Vilene in place. These stitches can be pulled out at the end.

6 Allowing ³⁄₄in (18mm) all round for turnings, cut the excess fabric away. Fold the fabric over onto the Vilene, pin and baste.

7 Place the lining fabric on top and work around the edge tucking and pinning the seam allowance underneath. Before stitching, fold the work into the shape of the bag to see whether it needs any easing or adjustment made to the lining. When it is correct, carefully oversew the edge with matching thread.

8 Fold up the sides to form the purse, oversewing them together making stab stitches through all thicknesses close to the edge. Cut two 40in (100cm) lengths each of red and navy stranded cotton, full thickness. Twist them together as you work around all the edges, oversewing them in place firmly with navy sewing thread. You can sew a press fastener or a small piece of Velcro to the flap and the front to close it.

Use this plan to position the design on fabric.

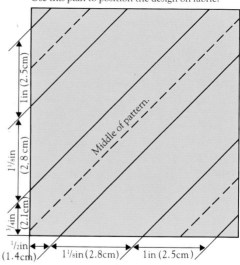

88

Trace and retrace this pattern as required.

KEY
A – Red 321, satin stitch   B – Navy 311, satin stitch   C – Navy, stem stitch

Something old . . .
something new

Bows and pearls

Pretty little bows in shadow embroidery have been worked around the edge of this simple, classic veil. The effect is achieved by working herringbone stitches, between the design lines, on the wrong side of the fabric. The stitches show as a soft image on the right side, outlined in backstitches. Small pearl beads are added to complete the design.

Materials
Ready-made veil, organza or chiffon (not net)
Tracing paper
DMC stranded embroidery cotton, ecru
Small seed pearl beads
Fine crewel needle; fine beading needle
Embroidery hoop
Sharply-pointed pencil
Transparent thread.

Preparation
1 Bind both rings of the embroidery hoop with bandage or soft bias binding. This must be tight and firmly secured with stitches to prevent the fine fabric from slipping in the frame.

2 Trace the bow from the picture 3¼in (8·5cm) apart from the picture on the next page and retrace, spacing bows. Draw a curved line between them for the pearl line.

3 Work basting stitches round the veil 1½in (40cm) from the edge, to position the embroidery.

4 Place the tracing on a hard surface and arrange the veil, wrong side up, on top so that the longer bow tail is on the basted line. You will need to weight down the veil to prevent it from slipping. With sharpened embroidery pencil trace the bows. Move the tracing and repeat the process until you have traced bows all round the veil.

5 Position the first motif centrally in the hoop. Tighten the screws carefully.

Working the embroidery
6 Use two strands of embroidery cotton. Begin by making two small backstitches on the line on the wrong side. Try to keep an even tension; if the work is pulled too tightly the fabric will pucker. If stitches are too loose they will catch.

7 Work closed herringbone stitches from side to side between the design lines, varying the length of stitches to fit the design.

8 Work the bows around the veil, checking to see that neat lines of running stitches are being achieved on the right side.

Adding the pearls
9 Thread the needle with transparent thread. Fasten the end at the side of the first bow. Knot on the wrong side. Bring the needle through and pick up one pearl, take the needle down close to the side of where the threads come through. Come up again ¼in (6mm) away to place the second pearl. Continue until all the pearls are sewn on.

10 The veil should be washed in lukewarm, detergent to remove the pencil traces. Rinse well, and spread flat on a large towel to dry.

When sewing on the beads, you may find that it helps to baste the fabric to a piece of brown paper so that you can see the design line more clearly. Spread beads on a piece of felt to prevent them rolling about.

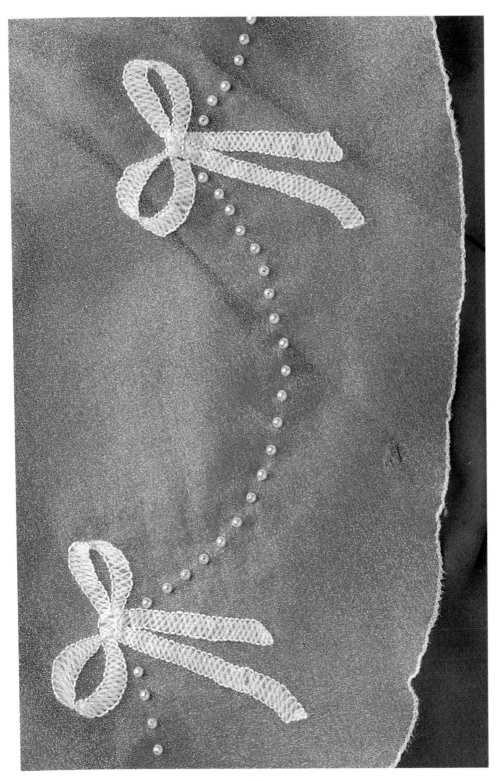

Something old, something new

A bow motif on the veil on page 93 could also be worked on the front of a prayer book cover for an elegant wedding accessory. The design is also suitable for a confirmation.

Materials
For a prayer book 3³/₄ × 5¹/₂ × 1¹/₂in (9.5 × 14 × 4cm). Adjust materials and size to suit your own requirements.
White, raw silk, (or a synthetic equivalent) 13¹/₂ × 10in (34 × 25cm)
DMC stranded embroidery cotton, Ecru
Mez Ophir Gold 0300
White sewing thread
Yellow embroidery pencil
Embroidery hoop
Vilene sew-in interlining 13¹/₂ × 10in (34 × 25cm).

Preparation
1 Pin the interlining to the wrong side of the silk fabric. Work a close zig-zag satin stitch around the edges through both layers.

2 Wrap the mounted fabric round the book (allowing a 2¹/₂in (6.5cm) flap inside the front cover) and mark the position for the bow using yellow embroidery pencil.

3 Trace the bow from page 93 and transfer in position. Place the fabric in a bound hoop (see page 92) with the bow placed centrally.

Working the embroidery
4 Using two strands of embroidery thread, work the design in close satin stitch. (The diagram shows the directions of the stitches.)

5 Outline the bow in small backstitches, using gold-thread.

Making the cover
6 Arrange the fabric on the book and fold the flaps to the inside. Mark with pins and remove the fabric from the book. Turn and stitch a narrow hem on the long edges of the flaps. Fold to the right side and stitch across the top and bottom edge of the flaps.

7 Turn the cover right side out. Couch two lengths of gold thread round the book edges (see picture).

> **Something blue . . .**
> If the prayer book is old and the embroidered cover is new, make sure of the bride's good luck by providing her with a blue keepsake. Embroider a small organdy bag with blue flowers, fill with dried lavender and tie the bag with very narrow ribbons. Sew the bag to a length of blue satin ribbon and pin to the petticoat waistband, so that the bag hangs just above the wedding dress hem.

Work satin stitches across the design lines, following the directions indicated.

Useful Addresses

DMC Creative World, Pullman Road, Wigston, Leicester LE8 2DY. Tel: 0533 811040.
DMC threads, embroidery fabrics, hoops, frames.

Stonehouse/Paterna, PO Box 13, Albion Mills, Wakefield, West Yorkshire, WF2 9SG. Tel: 0924 373456.

Dylon International Ltd, Lower Sydenham, London SE26 5HD.
Fabric paints and dyes.

Mail order suppliers:
Bedford Wool Shop, The Arcade, Bedford. Tel: 0234 55385.
Threads, fabrics, frames etc. (Personal shoppers also.)

Creativity of London, 35/37 New Oxford Street, London WC1A 1BH. Tel: 071 240 2945. (Personal shoppers also.)

Acknowledgments

The author thanks the following companies and individuals who assisted in the preparation of this book.

Wendy Walker, who worked my designs on pages 10, 24, 42, 54, 60, 80, 92, 94 and her own design on page 50.
Pat Round worked the designs on pages 16, 44 and 70.

Enid Gomes worked her design on pages 12 and 14.
Shirley Isaacs worked the design on page 18.
Erica Brisland worked the design on page 40.
DMC Creative World supplied the following designs: pages 34, 36 and 56.
Coats Needlecraft Design Studio supplied the designs on pages 24 and 28.
All other designs by the author.